JAZZ 2 TRUMPET

Transcribed by JOHN ROBERT BROWN

Indisputably one of the giants of jazz, Miles Davis has influenced the whole of jazz since World War Two. At several stages in his career Miles has discarded his previous approach to improvisation and taken up an entirely new direction. Time and again the resulting performances have changed the course of jazz history. To put it simply, Miles has repeatedly proved to be ahead of the game, and the man to watch.

This book © Copyright 1987

Warner Bros. Music Ltd
17 Berners Street
London W1P 3DD

Distributed by
International Music Publications
Southend Road
Woodford Green
Essex IG8 8HN

6·50

JAZZ 2 TRUMPET

FEATURING MILES DAVIS

Transcribed by **JOHN ROBERT BROWN**

These transcriptions cover the major part of Miles Davis' career, a period of nearly forty years from *The Birth Of The Cool* to *Tutu.* Trumpet parts are given at transposed (Bb) pitch, chord symbols and bass guide at concert pitch.

Saxophonist and arranger JOHN ROBERT BROWN is a Senior Lecturer on the full-time staff at the City of Leeds College of Music, where he has taught harmony and directed ensembles since 1975. He is a Vice-President of the Clarinet and Saxophone Society of Great Britain.
His other IMP publications include *Jazz Trumpet, Jazz Sax* books 1 and 2, and *Jazz Clarinet* books 1 and 2.

Foreword

BEBOP LIVES (Boplicity) is taken from the famous 1948 album THE BIRTH OF THE COOL. (Capitol T 1974 (11026)). This featured a nine-piece band of trumpet, trombone, French horn, tuba, alto saxophone, baritone saxophone, piano, bass and drums, and included several young musicians who were to become important names in the jazz world — Gerry Mulligan, Lee Konitz, John Lewis, Max Roach — playing arrangements by Gil Evans, Mulligan and Lewis. Bebop Lives was composed by Miles, who used his mother's name, Cleo Henry, as a pseudonym. Although the nonet only worked together for one fortnight in 1948 the arrangements were recorded in 1949 and 1950. These recordings were highly influential, and there is no doubt that the whole of the 1950s WEST COAST school of jazz was founded on the style pioneered by the nonet.

COMPULSION was recorded early in 1953, with a sextet that included Charlie Parker and Sonny Rollins. It has been reissued on MILES DAVIS COLLECTOR'S ITEMS (Prestige PR 24022).

MAIDS OF CADIZ, by Leo Delibes (1836-91) was included on the album MILES AHEAD (CBS 62496), with Miles on flugelhorn accompanied by a twenty piece orchestra under Gil Evans' direction. This was recorded in 1957, and the interest aroused by the LP was sufficient for Maids Of Cadiz to be issued as one side of a 45rpm single. In 1960 the orchestra and Miles were the subject of an American TV recording of some of the Miles Ahead items (plus a quintet version of So What). This is still occasionally transmitted on British television.

SID'S AHEAD was recorded in April 1958, and appears on the MILESTONES album (CS 9428), played by a small group containing Cannonball Adderley on alto saxophone and John Coltrane on tenor. Miles' solo is accompanied only by drums and bass.

BLUE IN GREEN, FLAMENCO SKETCHES, SO WHAT, ALL BLUES and FREDDIE FREELOADER comprise the whole of the album KIND OF BLUE (Columbia 8163) recorded in March 1959. This album has been described by Ian Carr in his book on Miles Davis (Paladin, 1984) as 'one of the seminal albums . . . one of the most enduring classics of jazz'. At the time of the preparation of this collection of transcriptions, nearly thirty years after the recording, the LP was still on sale in record shops.

SEVEN STEPS TO HEAVEN marks the record debut of one of Miles Davis' most talked about rhythm sections, the one containing Tony Williams, Herbie Hancock and Ron Carter, formed in 1963. These players developed a new role for the rhythm section, much more interactive than hitherto. Seven Steps To Heaven was recorded in May 1963 (Columbia CL 2051).

ESP has been called the best studio album since KIND OF BLUE. The album is represented in this collection by the title track, ESP, and by EIGHTY ONE, the latter an altered blues with rock rhythms alternating with a swing feel. This was a radical approach at the time of recording in January 1965. (Columbia 9150)

CIRCLE IN THE ROUND, from the album of the same name (CBS 88471), has a theme that is harmonised throughout in parallel fifths between and tenor. The resultant hollow, shiftless, sound, combined with the vague harmonic support, gives a curious mock-archaic sound.

STUFF, recorded in 1968, presents something of a transcriber's nightmare, because although the long theme is played four times, it is varied slightly each time, with bars removed and rhythms subtly changed. Only the first statement is represented here. This shifting and slightly 'off-square' character is echoed throughout the improvisation. In retrospect this aspect of the performance is of greater interest than the much vaunted borrowings from the pop music of the time. (Miles In The Sky CBS 85548).

SHH is the first track on the 1969 album IN A SILENT WAY (CBS 63630), an album which has received the highest critical acclaim. Ian Carr has called it 'artistically flawless'. This was the album which gave guitarist John McLaughlin crucial exposure. SHH is played over an unrelenting pedal D. Miles' solo is almost totally diatonic, and delightfully well-paced.

FAT TIME appeared on the album THE MAN WITH THE HORN (CBS 84708), which marked Miles' return from a six year sabbatical. The album was recorded in 1980/81. JEAN PIERRE dates from 1982, and uses a very similar band. The album was WE WANT MILES (CBS 88579).

THAT'S RIGHT is from DECOY (Columbia 25951), and was voted Jazz Album Of The Year 1984 by the readers of the leading jazz magazine DOWNBEAT. The album topped the sales charts, and was the subject of a four minute video. A nicely unexpected touch is the use of three four time in a rock context.

The following year 1985 saw the release of YOU'RE UNDER ARREST (CBS 26447) from which MS MORRISINE is transcribed. Another absolutely diatonic improvisation from Miles, which a three quaver 'signpost' ensemble figure marking each eight bars.

TUTU (Warner Bros 925 490-1) was released in the autumn of 1986. That year the readers of DOWNBEAT voted Miles' band BEST ELECTRIC JAZZ GROUP, but the magazine only awarded the album four out of a possible five stars. The title track TUTU was written by Marcus Miller, who stated that the tune came from a New Orleans beat that Miles felt comfortable with — a type of shuffle with a half-time backbeat.

Saxophonist and arranger JOHN ROBERT BROWN is a Senior Lecturer on the full-time staff at the City of Leeds College of Music, where he has taught harmony and directed ensembles since 1975. He is a Vice-President of the Clarinet and Saxophone Society of Great Britain. His other IMP publications include *Jazz Trumpet*, *Jazz Sax* books 1 and 2, and *Jazz Clarinet* books 1 and 2.

Bebop Lives
(Boplicity)

Music by
MILES DAVIS and RAY PASSMAN

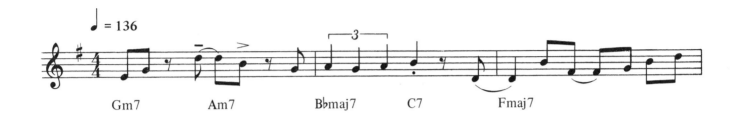

Copyright © 1986 Jazz Horn Music Inc./Warner Tamerlane Publ. Corp.
WARNER BROS. MUSIC LTD., 17 Berners Street, London W1P 3DD.
All Rights Reserved.

Bbmaj7 · · · Bbm7 · Eb7(#9#5)

Bbm7 · Eb7(#9#5) · Ab · Abm7 · Gm7 · C7(#11)

Gm7 · Am7 · Bbmaj7 · C7 · Fmaj7

Cm7 · F7(#9#5) · Bbmaj7 · Gm7 · Fmaj7/A

To Solos · Miles' Solo

Bbmaj7 · C7sus · F7b5 · F7

Bbm7 · Eb7 · Eb7(b9) · Abmaj7 · Dbmaj7

Ensemble

C7(b9) · F · Gm · Ab° · C · D° · Gm7 · Am

Bb Bᵒ C7 F F#ᵒ C7

F/A Gm7 Ab7 C7#11

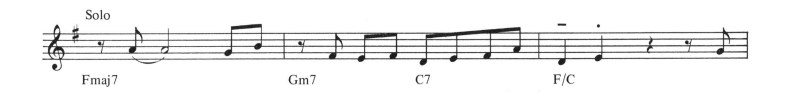

Solo

Fmaj7 Gm7 C7 F/C

Cm7 F7 Bb7(9) Gm7(9)

Gbmaj7 Fmaj7 F

Cm7 F7 Bb Bᵒ

F7 Bb7 Gm7 C7(#9) Fmaj7

All Blues

Music by
MILES DAVIS

Copyright © 1986 Jazz Horn Music Inc./WARNER TAMERLANE PUBL. CORP.
WARNER BROS. MUSIC LTD., 17 Berners Street, London W1P 3DD.
All Rights Reserved.

Blue In Green

Music by
MILES DAVIS

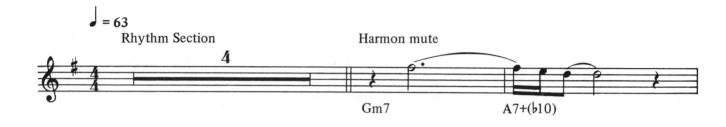

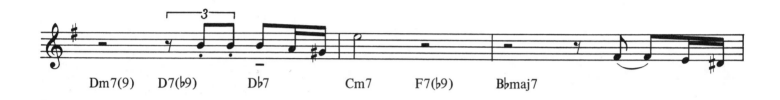

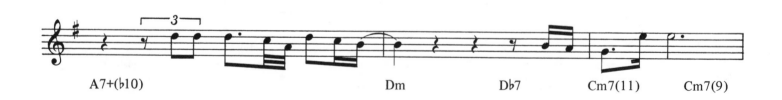

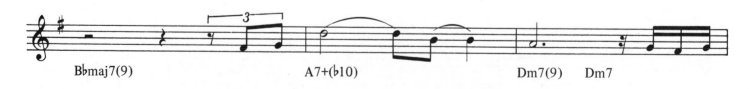

Copyright © 1986 JAZZ HORN MUSIC INC./WARNER TAMERLANE PUBL. CORP.
WARNER BROS. MUSIC LTD., 17 Berners Street, London W1P 3DD.
All Rights Reserved.

F7/B   E7+   Am7   Dm7   Gm7   Piano Solo

After Piano

Gm7   A7+(♭10)   Dm7(9)

Cm7   F7   B♭maj7   A7+

Dm7   F7(9)   E7(9)   Am7(9)   Dm

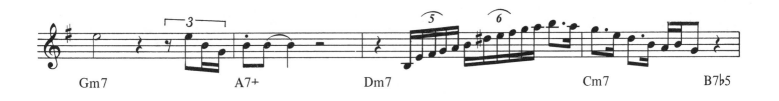

Gm7   A7+   Dm7   Cm7   B7♭5

B♭maj7   A7+(♭10)   Dm7   F7   E7

Piano concludes

Am7   Dm7

Circle In The Round

Music by
MILES DAVIS

Theme. Play three times
1. Lower part, tenor saxophone only
2. Duet as written, trumpet lead
3. Upper part only, trumpet and tenor saxophone in octaves

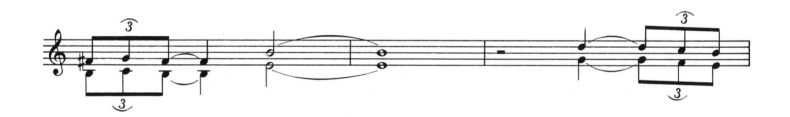

Miles' Solo

Copyright © 1986 Jazz Horn Music Inc./Warner Tamerlane Publ. Corp.
WARNER BROS. MUSIC LTD., 17 Berners Street, London W1P 3DD.
All Rights Reserved.

Compulsion

Music by
MILES DAVIS

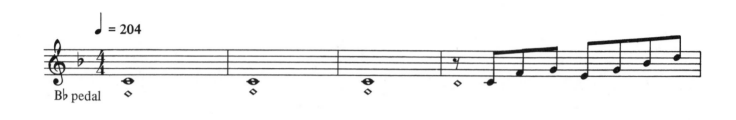

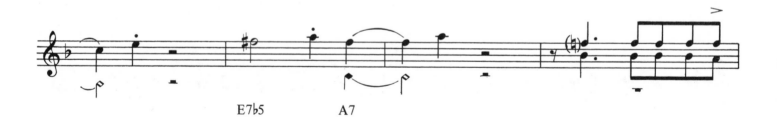

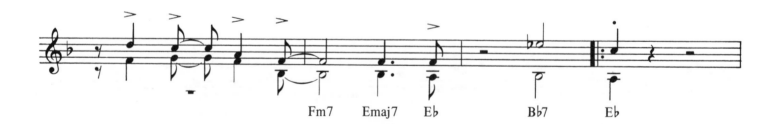

Copyright © 1986 JAZZ HORN MUSIC INC./WARNER TAMERLANE PUBL. CORP.
WARNER BROS. MUSIC LTD., 17 Berners Street, London W1P 3DD.
All Rights Reserved.

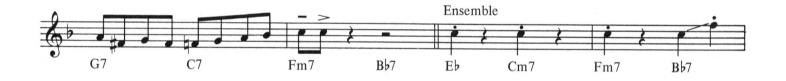

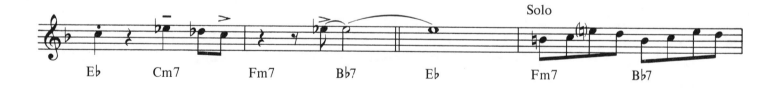

C7b5　　　　Fm7　　　　Bb7b5

Ensemble

Eb　　Cm7　　Fm7　　Bb7　　Eb　　Cm7

Fm7　　Bb7　　Eb　　**Solo**　　Fm7　　Bb7

Fm7　　Bb7　　Eb　　Eb

Fm7　　Bb　　Cm7　　Fm7　Bb7　　Eb　　Cm7

Fm7　　Bb7　　G7　　C7　　Fm7　　Bb7

Eb　　　　Fm7　　Bb7　　Cm7

Fm7　　Bb7　　　　Eb　　　　　Cm7　　　　Fm7　　　　　Bb7

Fm7　　Bb7　　　　Eb　　　　　　　　Bbm7

Eb7　　　　　　　　Abm7　　　　　　Db7

Gm　　　　　　C7b5　　　　　Fm7

Bb7b5　　　　　　Eb　　　　　Fm7　　　　Bb7

Eb　　Cm7　　　　Fm7　　　Bb7　　Eb　　　　Cm7

Fm7　　　Bb7　　　　Fm7　　Bb7　　Eb

Eighty One

Music by
MILES DAVIS and RON CARTER

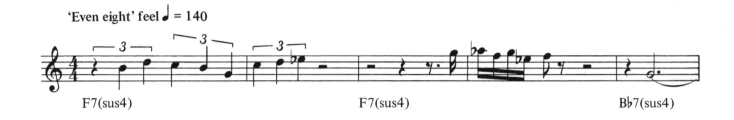

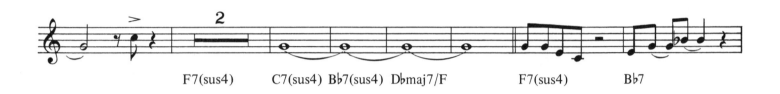

Miles' Solo

Copyright © 1986 JAZZ HORN MUSIC INC./WARNER TAMERLANE PUBL. CORP.
WARNER BROS. MUSIC LTD., 17 Berners Street, London W1P 3DD.
All Rights Reserved.

E.S.P.

Music by
MILES DAVIS and WAYNE SHORTER

$\quad = 288$

Theme — unison trumpet and tenor saxophone

Copyright © 1986 JAZZ HORN MUSIC INC./WARNER TAMERLANE PUBL. CORP.
WARNER BROS. MUSIC LTD., 17 Berners Street, London W1P 3DD.
All Rights Reserved.

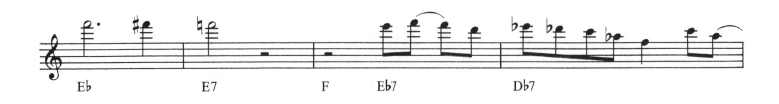

E7   F7

E7

E♭7   D7   E♭

E7   Fmaj7   E♭7   D♭7

C7   D♭7   G♭7   F7

E7   F7

E7   E♭7

Solo continues

Flamenco Sketches

Music by
MILES DAVIS

Copyright © 1986 Jazz Horn Music Inc./Warner Tamerlane Publ. Corp.
WARNER BROS. MUSIC LTD., 17 Berners Street, London W1P 3DD.
All Rights Reserved.

Fat Time

Music by
MILES DAVIS

Copyright © 1986 JAZZ HORN MUSIC INC./WARNER TAMERLANE PUBL. CORP.
WARNER BROS. MUSIC LTD., 17 Berners Street, London W1P 3DD.
All Rights Reserved.

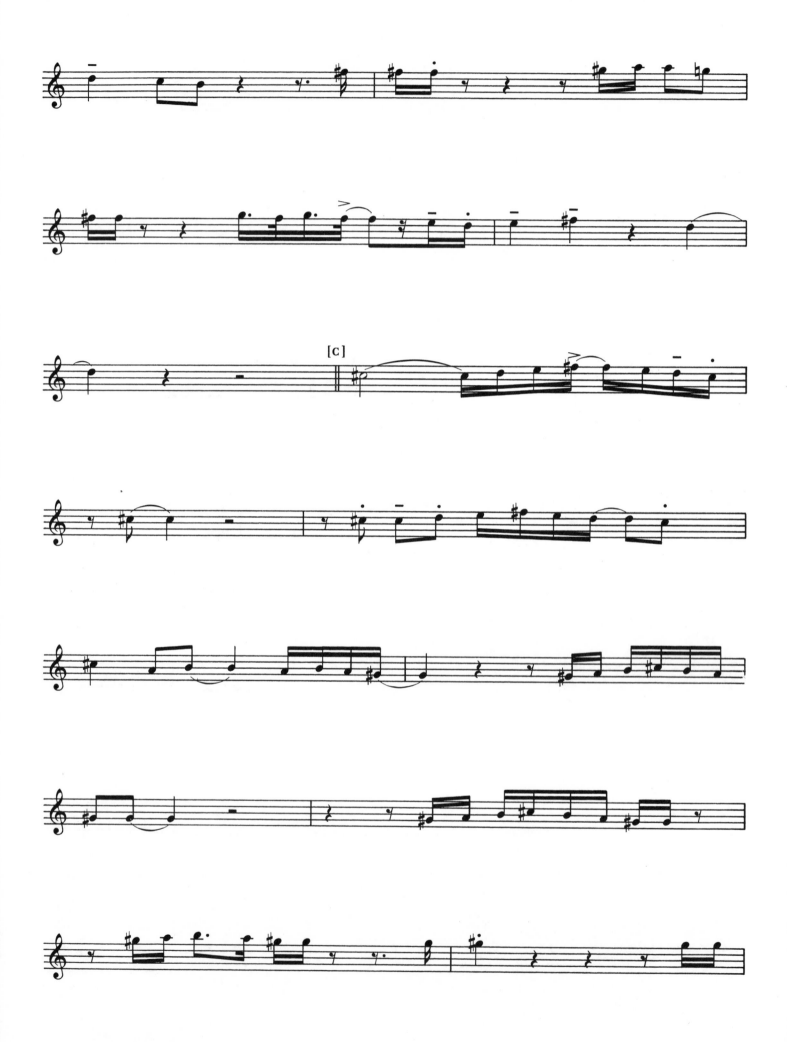

No chord symbols are given because the accompaniment is mostly bass and drums. The key scheme of the accompaniment (concert pitch) is:—

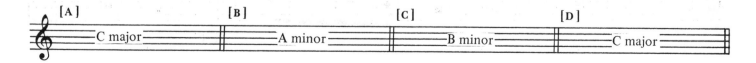

Freddie Freeloader

Music by
MILES DAVIS

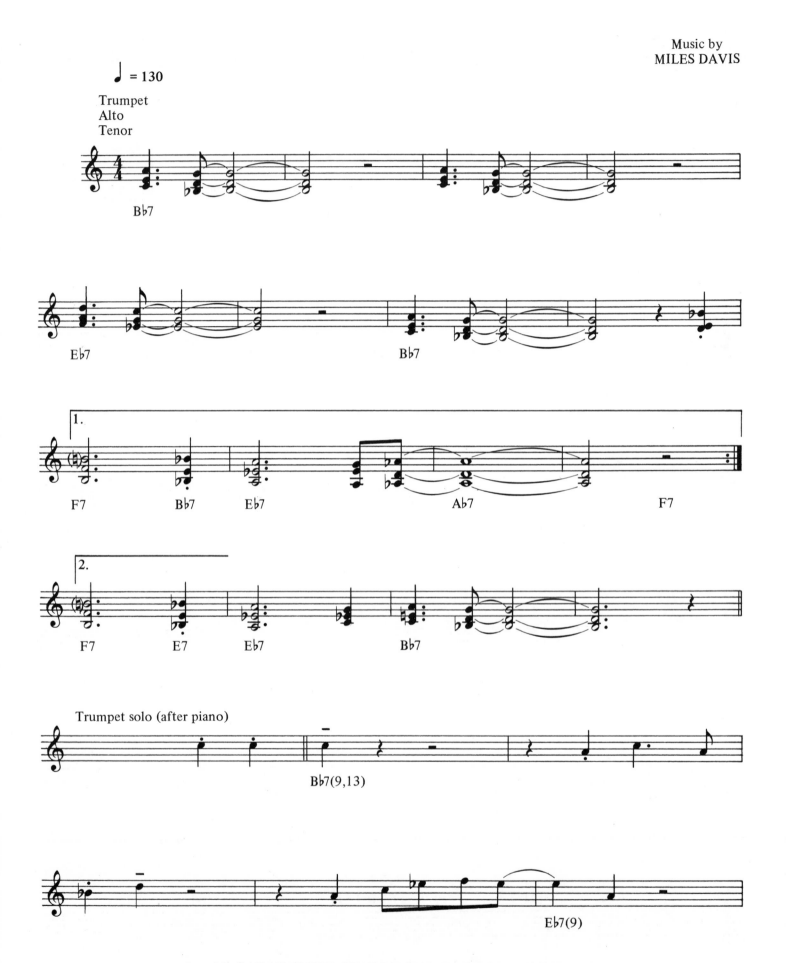

Copyright © 1986 JAZZ HORN MUSIC INC./WARNER TAMERLANE PUBL. CORP.
WARNER BROS. MUSIC LTD., 17 Berners Street, London W1P 3DD.
All Rights Reserved.

Jean Pierre

Music by
MILES DAVIS

Copyright © 1986 JAZZ HORN MUSIC INC./WARNER TAMERLANE PUBL. CORP.
WARNER BROS. MUSIC LTD., 17 Berners Street, London W1P 3DD.
All Rights Reserved.

Repeat [A] to [B] section then guitar solos, etc.

Shhh

Music by
MILES DAVIS

♩ = 132

Drums, after pause Bass. This bass pattern continues throughout Solo (concert pitch).

Trumpet (B♭ pitch)

Copyright © 1986 JAZZ HORN MUSIC INC./WARNER TAMERLANE PUBL. CORP.
WARNER BROS. MUSIC LTD., 17 Berners Street, London W1P 3DD.
All Rights Reserved.

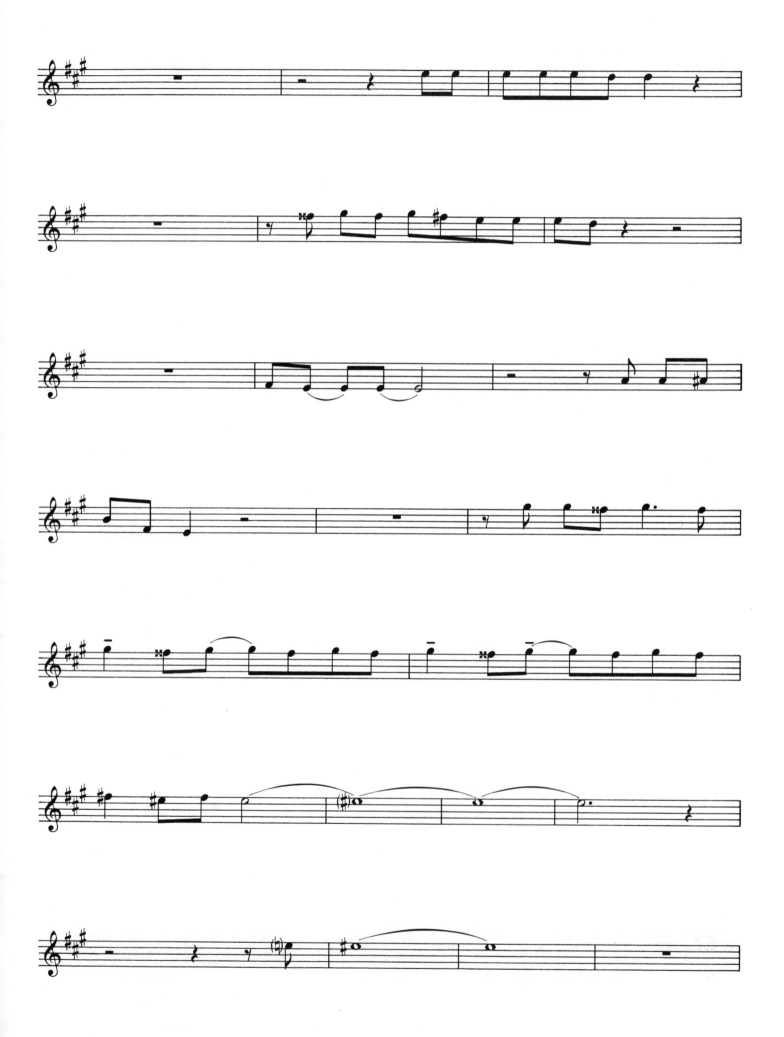

The Maids Of Cadiz

Music by
DELIBES

trad. arr: JOHN ROBERT BROWN

Gm   Gm/F   E♭

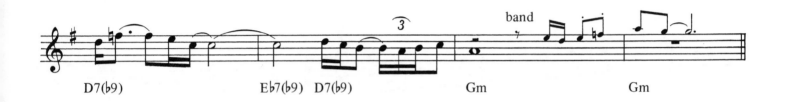

D7(♭9)   E♭7(♭9)   D7(♭9)   Gm   Gm

Gm   Gm/F   Em7♭5   G° A♭° A° B♭°

G7   B♭maj7   A7   A♭7(♭5)   D♭7(♯11 9)   Cm   Cm♯5

Cm6   Cm♯5   Cm   D7(♯9♭9)   A♭   A   B♭m7(♭5)

B♭   F7   G♭7   B7   B♭maj7   F♯7/B♭

Copyright © 1986 WARNER BROS. MUSIC LTD.
WARNER BROS. MUSIC LTD., 17 Berners Street, London W1P 3DD.
All Rights Reserved.

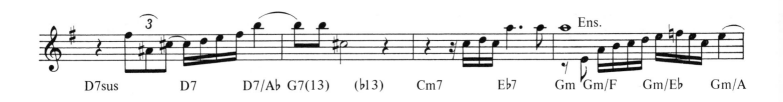

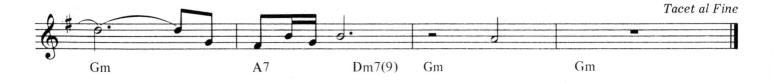

Ms. Morrisine

Music by
M. TYNES IRVING, MILES DAVIS
and ROBERT IRVING III

Copyright © 1986 JAZZ HORN MUSIC INC./VITASIA PUBLISHING CO./WARNER TAMERLANE PUBL. CORP.
WARNER BROS. MUSIC LTD., 17 Berners Street, London W1P 3DD.
All Rights Reserved.

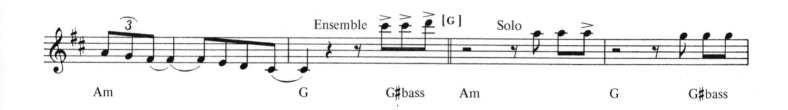

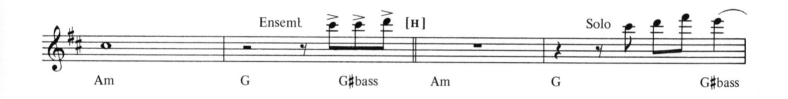

Am   G   G#bass   Am   G   G#bass

[K]

Am   G   G#bass   Am   G   G#bass

Am   G   G#bass   Am   G   G#bass

[L]

Am   G   G#bass   Am   G   G#bass

Am   G   G#bass   Am   G   G#bass

[M]

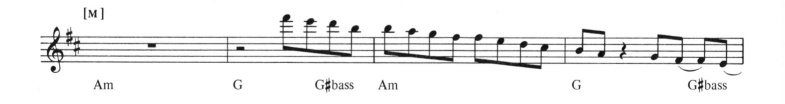

Am   G   G#bass   Am   G   G#bass

Am   G   G#bass   Am   G

Seven Steps To Heaven

Music by
MILES DAVIS and VICTOR STANLEY FELDMAN

Copyright © 1986 JAZZ HORN MUSIC INC./WARNER TAMERLANE PUBL. CORP.
WARNER BROS. MUSIC LTD., 17 Berners Street, London W1P 3DD.
All Rights Reserved.

Eb7   G7   C

Dm7   G7   C   Fm7   Bb7

Eb7   Abm7   Db7   Gb7   C7

F   Em7b5   A7   Dm

Gm7   C7   Eb7   C7

F   Em7b5   A7   Dm7

Gm7   C7   Eb7   C7

F   Em7♭5   A7   Dm7

Gm7   C7   E♭7   G7

C   Dm7   G7   C   Fm7   B♭7

E♭7   A♭m7   D♭7   G♭7   C7

F   Em7♭5   A7   Dm7

Gm7   C7   E♭7   C7

F   Em7♭5   A7   Dm7

Gm7　C7　Eb7　C7

F　Em7b5　A7　Dm7

Gm7　C7　Eb7　G7

C　Dm7　G7　C　Fm7　Bb7

Eb7　Abm7　D7　Gb7　C7

F　Em7b5　A7　Dm　Gm7

C7　Eb7　C7

Sid's Ahead

Music by
MILES DAVIS

Copyright © 1986 Jazz Horn Music Inc./WARNER TAMERLANE PUBL. CORP.
WARNER BROS. MUSIC LTD., 17 Berners Street, London W1P 3DD.
All Rights Reserved.

To Solos
original has bass and drums
accompaniment only

Miles' Solo

D7

F7   C7   F7   C7

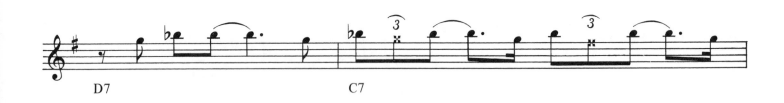

D7   C7

Bb7

D7   C7

D7

F7

So What

Music by
MILES DAVIS

♩ = 136

Trumpet version
B♭ pitch

[A] With ensemble

Dm7

Copyright © 1986 JAZZ HORN MUSIC INC./WARNER TAMERLANE PUBL. CORP.
WARNER BROS. MUSIC LTD., 17 Berners Street, London W1P 3DD.
All Rights Reserved.

So What

Music by
MILES DAVIS

Copyright © 1986 Jazz Horn Music Inc./WARNER TAMERLANE PUBL. CORP.
WARNER BROS. MUSIC LTD., 17 Berners Street, London W1P 3DD.
All Rights Reserved.

That's Right

Music by
MILES DAVIS and JOHN SCOFIELD

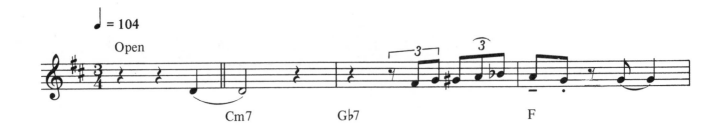

Copyright © 1986 JAZZ HORN MUSIC INC./WARNER TAMERLANE PUBL. CORP.
WARNER BROS. MUSIC LTD., 17 Berners Street, London W1P 3DD.
All Rights Reserved.

G bass   F# bass   F7   Cm7/F   Cm7

Cm7/F   Cm7

F7sus4

Cm7   F7sus4/C

Cm7/F   F7sus4   Cm7

Cm7

F# bass   F7   no chord   C7sus

Cm7   F7(9)   Cm7

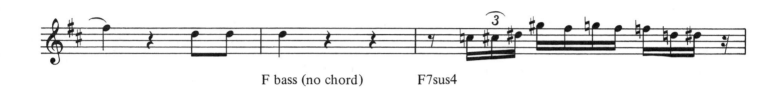

F bass (no chord)   F7sus4

C7sus4   F7(9)

C7sus4   C7(♭9)sus4

F7sus4

flurry

Cm7(add 4)

F7sus   Cm7

Tutu

Music by
MARCUS MILLER

Copyright © 1986 THRILLER MILLER MUSIC.
MCA MUSIC LTD., 139 Piccadilly, London W1V 9FH.

73

Band continues with repeat of 14 bars from [B], with trumpet fills.

Stuff

Music by
MILES DAVIS

'Even eight' feel ♩ = 116

Db7(#9)   B7

Bb7   C7

Db7

E7#11   Bb7   G

D7

Copyright © 1986 JAZZ HORN MUSIC INC./WARNER TAMERLANE PUBL. CORP
WARNER BROS. MUSIC LTD., 17 Berners Street, London W1P 3DD.
All Rights Reserved.

G

Play four times Miles' Solo

Db7(#9)   Db7(#9)   D7

C7   B7   Bb7

C7   Bb7

C7   Db7

C7   Db7   C7

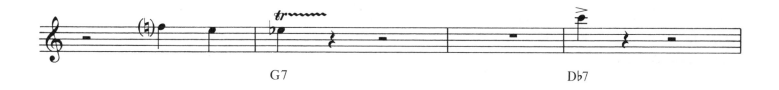

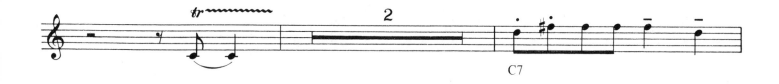

Printed by Watkiss Studios Ltd., Biggleswade, Beds. 6/87